SCHOLASTIC

Grades 4–8

5-Minute Grammar Practice

180 Quick & Motivating Activities Students Can Use to Practice Essential Grammar Skills—Every Day of the School Year

Judith Bauer Stamper

Edited by Mela Ottaiano
Cover designed by Brian LaRossa and illustrated by Jim Paillot
Interior designed by Holly Grundon and illustrated by Mike Moran
Interactive whiteboard activities designed by Jason Robinson and illustrated by Jim Paillot

ISBN: 978-0-545-29056-2
Copyright © 2003, 2011 by Judith Bauer Stamper
All rights reserved. Published by Scholastic Inc.
Printed in the U.S.A.

1 2 3 4 5 6 7 8 9 10   40   17 16 15 14 13 12 11

New York • Toronto • London • Auckland • Sydney
Mexico City • New Delhi • Hong Kong • Buenos Aires

Teaching *Resources*

Contents

Introduction

Grammar is one of those important subjects that many students find difficult to learn. One solution is to offer students grammar practice in small doses. This product is designed to do just that. Each of the 180 grammar activities should take the typical student only five minutes to complete. Students get quick and much-needed practice in parts of speech, sentence structure, capitalization, punctuation, and much more.

What's Inside This Product

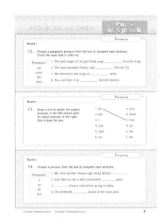

Inside the book, you'll find 180 reproducible grammar exercises. They are specifically tailored to introduce kids to the power of grammar, reinforce language-arts skills, and elicit a few smiles, to boot. The companion CD features the same 180 exercises on individual pages, intended for use with a Promethean ActivBoard.

How to Use the Resource

Here is one way to get the most out of the exercises:

- Select the grammar skill you'd like students to work on.
- Reproduce a corresponding page in the book, clip apart, and distribute the activity to students.
- Give students five minutes to complete it independently.
- Display the activity on the board and call volunteers to answer the problems.
- Have students check their own work against the board.

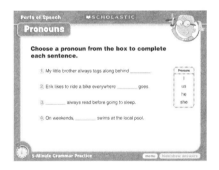

Another approach is to first model one of the exercises on the interactive whiteboard. Follow up by distributing a reproducible version of a similar exercise. Students can complete the exercise independently or work in pairs.

How to Use the CD Files

The companion CD includes ready-to-go Flipchart files created in ActivInspire. Download the files onto the computer that connects to the interactive whiteboard. Use the menu to select the activity you'd like to use.

Students can use the pen function to write in or circle answers. Where appropriate, there are also many opportunities to drag and drop answers from a bank of options. If the drag function is not enabled, this indicates that students must rewrite the word in some way, such as adding capitalization or changing it to a plural.

Once satisfied that their answers are correct, students simply click on a button to reveal the answer.

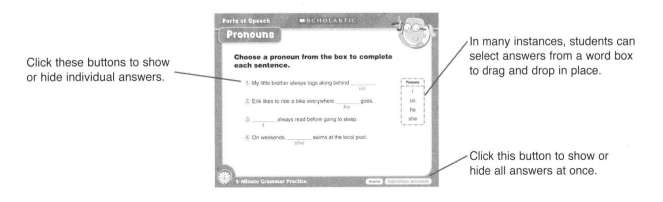

Click these buttons to show or hide individual answers.

In many instances, students can select answers from a word box to drag and drop in place.

Click this button to show or hide all answers at once.

Tech Tips

If you don't already have ActivInspire software, you can access a free personal version after registering with Promethean Planet (www.prometheanplanet.com). For more information, click the links you'll find on the PDF included on the CD.

If you are still getting the hang of your ActivBoard, be sure to look at the tips on Promethean Planet. However, the following is an overview of the main ActivInspire features to use with these activities.

 In the **Pin Toolbox**, you will find the Page Browser and the Notes Browser.

 Use the **Page Browser** to call up the page you'd like to display.

 In the **Notes Browser** you will find the activity number that corresponds to the activity in the book. It will also indicate any special information related to that page.

 Use the **Previous/Next Page** icons to navigate between pages.

 The **Select** function works like a typical computer mouse when you navigate the screen.

 Use the **Pen** function to write directly on the screen in digital ink. You may change the color and size of the "ink." Avoid writing answers in green as this color is used for the on-screen annotations.

 Use the **Highlighter** function to call attention to key text. (You also may change its color and size.)

 Like its old-fashioned counterpart, the **Eraser** removes unwanted writing. It will work on text and lines created with the pen function. It will not work on typed text or art objects.

 The **Clear** function makes it easy to clean up the page. Select from the menu the type of writing, text, or art you'd like to remove.

 If students are adding text to a small field or simply prefer typing to writing freehand, use the **On-screen Keyboard**. You can access it through the Desktop Tools menu.

 Rather than using the undo command to clear annotation one by one, you may click the **Reset Page** icon to clear all marks at once.

Parts of Speech

Nouns

Name: _____

1. Decide if each noun is a person, place, or thing.
Sort them in the chart below.

city	fans	baseball	girl	coach
net	outfield	Chicago	medal	hurdle
Europe	runner	Venus Williams

Person	Place	Thing

Nouns

Name: _____

2. Find three nouns in each sentence and circle them.

1. My brother plays soccer and tennis.

2. The batter hit the ball out of the park.

3. The team ran onto the court as the fans cheered.

Nouns

Name: _____

3. Underline the common noun and circle the proper noun in each sentence.

1. I think Michael Jordan is the greatest basketball player ever.

2. The best runner came from Kenya.

3. Mia Hamm inspires young female athletes.

Nouns

Name: _____

4. Circle the first letter of each noun in the sports report below. Then write these letters in order to spell out the names of three sports.

Heroes Against the Odds

The crowd screamed for Kyle Ellis as the youngster
led his team, the Eagles, to win the nationals in Newport.
An invitation to play soccer here had been hard
to get. But the team set a record for young athletes.
And they won the championship because of Kyle.

Sport 1: ____ ____ ____ ____ ____ ____

Sport 2: ____ ____ ____ ____ ____ ____

Sport 3: ____ ____ ____ ____ ____

Singular & Plural Nouns

Name: _____

5. Write **S** if the noun is singular and **P** if it is plural.

_____ 1. teammates   _____ 5. base   _____ 9. sheep

_____ 2. captain   _____ 6. guard   _____ 10. gym

_____ 3. fouls   _____ 7. jerseys

_____ 4. skate   _____ 8. racket

Singular & Plural Nouns

Name: _____

6. Circle the noun in each sentence. Then write **S** if it is singular and **P** if it is plural.

_____ 1. The zoo was crowded.

_____ 2. People were everywhere.

_____ 3. I saw a huge elephant.

Singular & Plural Nouns

Name: _____

7. Make each of the boldfaced nouns plural by adding -s or -es.

1. I went to the zoo with my **brother**____ and sister.

2. We saw **fox**____ in the forest habitat.

3. Zebras hid behind **bush**____ in the African habitat.

4. My favorite animals were the **gorilla**____.

Hint

Add –es to nouns that end in s, ch, sh, x, or z.

Singular & Plural Nouns

Name: _____

8. Complete each sentence with the plural form of a noun from the box.

Nouns
monkey
knife
key
leaf

1. A zookeeper opened the lion's cage with a set of _____.

2. The panda chewed on the bamboo _____.

3. The zoo's cooks cut up vegetables with sharp _____.

4. We went to see the _____ after we saw the gorillas.

Singular & Plural Nouns

Name: _____

9. Draw a line to connect the singular noun in the left column with its plural In the right column.

1. tooth	a. geese
2. woman	b. halves
3. half	c. mice
4. goose	d. teeth
5. mouse	e. women

Singular & Plural Nouns

Name: _____

10. Rewrite the sentences below, making all the singular nouns plural.

1. The lion walked back and forth in the cage.

   _____

2. The fox ran past the tree and into the bush.

   _____

3. The child tossed a ball into the hoop.

   _____

Pronouns

Name: _____

11. Choose a pronoun from the box that can replace the underlined words in the sentences below. Write it in the blank.

Pronouns

they

it

he

1. <u>Tim</u> wants to become a member of a rock band. _____

2. <u>The guitar</u> is his favorite instrument. _____

3. <u>His friends</u> are good musicians, too. _____

Pronouns

Name: _____

12. Choose a possessive pronoun from the box to complete each sentence. Circle the noun that it refers to.

Pronouns
our
your
her
their

1. The lead singer of the girl band sang _____ favorite song.

2. The band members finally had _____ first hit CD.

3. We listened to the song on _____ radio.

4. You can hear it on _____ favorite station.

Pronouns

Name: _____

13. Draw a line to match the subject pronoun in the left column with its object pronoun in the right. One is done for you.

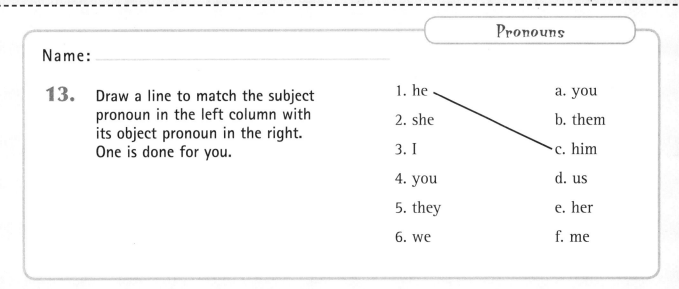

1. he   a. you

2. she   b. them

3. I   c. him

4. you   d. us

5. they   e. her

6. we   f. me

Pronouns

Name: _____

14. Choose a pronoun from the box to complete each sentence.

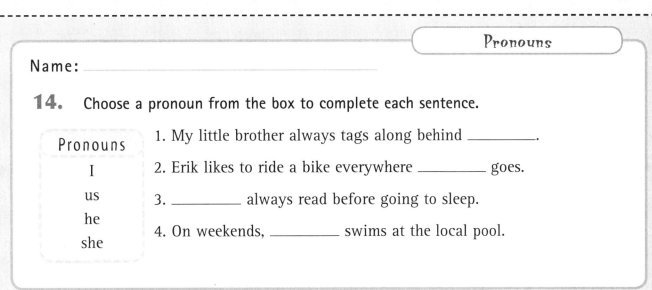

Pronouns
I
us
he
she

1. My little brother always tags along behind _____.

2. Erik likes to ride a bike everywhere _____ goes.

3. _____ always read before going to sleep.

4. On weekends, _____ swims at the local pool.

Name: _____

15. Write whether each pronoun is singular or plural. In the last column, write a sentence using a noun that could replace the pronoun.

Pronoun	Singular or Plural?	Sentence
She		
They		
His		
We		

Name: _____

16. Fill in the correct pronoun from the box in each blank. Make sure it agrees in number and gender to the noun it replaces.

Teresa Lopez is the editor of our school newspaper.

_____ makes sure the newspaper comes out on time

every week. Reporters get _____ assignments from

Teresa. They hand _____ the articles to print.

Because of Teresa, the newspaper is a big success.

_____ is read by everyone in school.

Pronouns

their

it

her

she

Parts of Speech

Pronouns

Name: _____

17. Circle the singular pronoun in each sentence below. Then rewrite the sentence using a plural pronoun. Change the verb as necessary.

1. I like the comics section of the newspaper best.

   _____

2. Teresa asked her to cover the soccer game.

   _____

3. He writes the humor column for the newspaper.

   _____

Pronouns

Name: _____

18. Write the possessive pronoun that can replace the underlined word or words.

1. "Where is <u>Bill's</u> article about the game?" Teresa asked.   _____

2. "I think it is in <u>Bill's and my</u> cubby," Jody answered.   _____

3. "Is <u>Jody's</u> article ready?" Teresa asked next.   _____

4. "Yes, but I still have to write <u>the article's</u> headline," Jody said.   _____

Subject/Object Nouns & Pronouns

Name: _____

19. Underline the nouns that are the subjects of the verbs below.

1. The first airplane was invented in 1903.

2. Wilbur and Orville Wright flew it at Kitty Hawk, North Carolina.

3. Today jets fly all around the world.

Name: _____

20. Fill in the blanks with nouns that are objects of the verbs in the story below.

My Dad drove our _____ to the airport. We checked our _____ inside the terminal. We bought _____ and _____ to take on the flight. We boarded the _____. We played _____ and read _____ during the flight. It was a lot of fun!

Name: _____

21. Fill in the chart with the missing subject and object pronoun pairs.

Subject	Object
I	
	you
	him
she	
it	
	us
they	

Name: _____

22. Circle the pronoun in each sentence. Write S if it is a subject pronoun and O if it is an object pronoun.

_____ 1. We learned about Amelia Earhart in history class.

_____ 2. People all over the world admired her.

_____ 3. She was the first woman to fly across the Atlantic Ocean.

Parts of Speech

Subject/Object Nouns & Pronouns

Name: _____

23. Rewrite each sentence replacing a noun with a pronoun.

1. Wilbur and Orville Wright were aviation pioneers.

   _____

2. Sally Ride was the first American woman in space.

   _____

3. Neil Armstrong walked on the moon.

   _____

Collective & Possessive Nouns

Name: _____

24. Underline the collective nouns in the following sentences.

1. The audience cheered for the school band.

2. The choir sang the national anthem.

3. Our class sat in the front of the auditorium.

Hint
A collective noun names a group of people, animals, or things.

Collective & Possessive Nouns

Name: _____

25. Match the collective noun on the left with the group of animals it describes.

1. flock   a. bees

2. school   b. lions

3. swarm   c. birds

4. herd   d. fish

5. pride   e. buffalo

Name: _____

26. Add an 's to make a singular noun possessive. Add just an apostrophe (') to a plural noun that ends with s.

Singular Nouns	Possessive	Plural Nouns	Possessive
hamster		dogs	
quarterback		runners	
bike		motorcycles	
girl		boys	

Name: _____

27. Complete each sentence using the possessive form of the noun.

1. The (mice) _____ presence bothered the cat.

2. My mother studied the (geese) _____ migration.

3. There were three windows in the (children) _____ tree house.

Hint

If a plural noun does not end in s, add 's to make it possessive.

Name: _____

28. Underline the possessive noun in each sentence.
Write S if it is singular and P if it's plural.

_____ 1. The coaches' meeting was on Tuesday.

_____ 2. The boys' uniforms were gold and black.

_____ 3. The tournament was for the women's soccer teams.

_____ 4. The referee's whistle blew, and the game began.

Verbs

Name: _____

29. Circle the verb, or action word, in each sentence.

1. The wind ripped branches from the trees.

2. Rain pounded on the roof.

3. Thunder rumbled through the air.

Verbs

Name: _____

30. Write a verb in the blank to complete each sentence.

1. Heavy snow _____ during a blizzard.

2. Strong winds _____ the snow into drifts.

3. Ice _____ the roads and makes them slippery.

Verbs

Name: _____

31. Circle the helping verb in each sentence. Underline the main verb.

1. The tornado is moving in our direction.

2. The trees are bending in the wind.

3. We can hear the tornado's loud winds.

Verbs

Name: _____

32. Circle the word that is a form of the verb *to be* in each sentence. Then write whether it is a main verb or a helping verb.

1. They are survivors of Hurricane Gloria. _____

2. I am volunteering to help victims of the hurricane. _____

3. Almost two thousand families are homeless. _____

Name: _____

33. Circle the first letter of each verb below. Write them on the lines to spell out another word for tornado.

The storm tore through the town. It wrecked cars on the roads. It interrupted the electricity. Residents streamed into the town's storm shelter. They trembled with fear. After the storm, they emerged. They ran to their damaged homes.

___ ___ ___ ___ ___ ___ ___ ___

Name: _____

34. Write whether each sentence takes place in the past, present, or future.

1. I ride my bike to school.   _____

2. I walked to school when I was younger.   _____

3. I will ride a skateboard next year.   _____

Name: _____

35. Circle the verb in the present tense.

1. Today, many people (ride / rode) on skateboards.

2. Skateboarders (will perform / perform) amazing tricks.

3. A skateboard (took / takes) you anywhere.

Verb Tenses

Name: _____

36. Rewrite each sentence using a verb in the past tense.

1. The boy falls off his skateboard.

_____

2. Luckily, he is wearing safety equipment.

_____

3. He gets back up and skates on down the street.

_____

Verb Tenses

Name: _____

37. Add the word *will* in front of each verb to turn it into the future tense.

A thousand years from now, people _____ move from place to place in amazing ways. To get to school, children _____ jump onto their power scooters. The scooters _____ fly them to school. To go on field trips, students _____ climb into special transporters that _____ beam them to distant places. The future _____ be a lot of fun!

Irregular Verbs

Name: _____

38. Fill in the past-tense form of each verb. Then write a sentence using the past-tense verbs.

Verb	Past Tense	Sentence
sit		
find		
tell		

Name: _____

39. Write the past tense of the verb in parentheses to complete each sentence.

1. Our class (go) _____ to the play *Annie* last week.

2. The actors (sing) _____ songs and danced.

3. Annie's dog, Sandy, (steal) _____ the show.

Name: _____

40. Complete each sentence with the past-tense form of a verb from the box.

Verbs
speak
keep
see
fly

1. Last night, we _____ a movie that was set in England.

2. The actors _____ with English accents.

3. The characters _____ planes during World War II.

4. They _____ the Nazis from invading England.

Name: _____

41. Fill in the missing forms of the verbs in the chart. One is done for you.

Present	Past	Past Participle
see	saw	seen
speak		spoken
	rang	
do		

Parts of Speech

Irregular Verbs

Name: _____

42. Write sentences using the verbs listed.

1. gave _____

2. taken _____

3. wore _____

Adjectives

Name: _____

43. Circle each adjective below. Then check whether it tells what kind, how many, or which one.

	What kind?	How many?	Which one?
huge snakes			
that tree			
four birds			
green leaves			

Adjectives

Name: _____

44. Fill in each blank with an adjective that tells what kind.

We climbed into the _____ canoe and paddled down the river. In the water, we saw piranha fish snapping their _____ teeth. On the shore, we saw a _____ snake hanging from a _____ tree branch. We were having a _____ adventure in the rain forest.

Name: _____

45. Circle the adjectives that tell how many or how much below.

1. The rain forest has three layers.

2. The top layer gets the most light.

3. The two bottom layers have animals.

4. Several monkeys swing on branches and vines.

Name: _____

46. Fill in each blank with an adjective from the box that tells which one.

Adjectives
this
these
that
those

1. First, we'll cross _____ river; then we'll cross _____ one.

2. I'm not afraid of _____ little insects on my arm.

3. But I'm scared of _____ big ones on the wall.

Name: _____

47. Circle the five adverbs in the story.

Hint

An adverb describes or tells about a verb.

At lunchtime, students at our school quickly rush to the cafeteria. They stand impatiently in line. That's because the food in our cafeteria tastes great. The sandwiches are piled high with meat. And the pizza never disappoints us!

Parts of Speech

Adverbs

Name: _____

48. Fill in each blank with an adverb that answers the question "how?"

1. I was so hungry that I _____ picked up four pieces of pizza.

2. My stomach was growling _____.

3. I stared at the slices _____.

4. Then I _____ gobbled down all the pizza.

Adverbs

Name: _____

49. Circle the adverb in each sentence. Check whether each adverb answers the question "where?" or "when?"

	Where?	When?
1. The cafeteria served tacos yesterday.	_____	_____
2. The smell of tacos spread everywhere.	_____	_____
3. We ran downstairs to the cafeteria.	_____	_____
4. We always love to eat tacos!	_____	_____

Adverbs

Name: _____

50. Place these adverbs in the chart under the question they answer about a verb.

near	gently	fast	never	often	here
slowly	inside	tomorrow	up	finally	easily

How?	Where?	When?

Name: _____

51. Circle the four adverbs that describe adjectives in the story below.

I have an extremely unusual pet. It is a really cute snake named Slinky. Slinky is a very large boa constrictor. My little sister thinks Slinky is too gross for words!

Name: _____

52. Use the adverbs in the box to fill in the blanks and describe other adverbs.

Adverbs
quite
very
too
extremely

1. My snake moves _____ slowly.
2. His tongue flickers out _____ quickly.
3. My sister screams _____ loudly.
4. She runs away _____ fast.

Name: _____

53. You can change many adjectives into adverbs by adding -ly. Fill in the chart below.

Adjective	+ ly = Adverb	Adjective	+ ly = Adverb
soft		foolish	
loud		beautiful	
awkward		happy	

Name: _____

54. Circle the adverb in each sentence. Then write whether it describes a verb, an adverb, or an adjective.

1. Snakes swallow their food greedily.   _____

2. They are extremely fast eaters.   _____

3. Their food moves very slowly into their stomachs.   _____

Parts of Speech

Adverbs

Name: _____

55. Match the adverb on the left with one on the right with an opposite meaning.

1. extremely	a. quietly
2. rapidly	b. rudely
3. loudly	c. slightly
4. gently	d. slowly
5. politely	e. strongly

Comparing Adjectives & Adverbs

Name: _____

56. Fill in each blank with *more* or *most*.

1. Dan has _____ baseball trading cards than Ted.

2. His cousin Gwen has even _____ Yankee cards than Dan.

3. The person in school with the _____ trading cards is Tom.

Hint

Use *more* to compare two things; use *most* to compare three or more things.

Comparing Adjectives & Adverbs

Name: _____

57. Add *-er* or the word *more* to compare two things. Add *-est* or *most* to compare three or more things.

Adjective	Comparing Two	Comparing Three or More
fast		
athletic		
expensive		
new		

Name: _____

58. Add *-er* or *-est* to the adverbs below.

1. Of all the runners, Lisa tried hard_____ to win.

2. The high jumper from our school leaped high_____ than the jumper from San Jose.

3. The last runner in the four-man relay ran fast_____ of all.

4. Our coach yelled loud_____ than the coach from San Jose.

Name: _____

59. Add *-er* or *more* to an adverb to compare two actions. Add *-est* or *most* to an adverb to compare three or more actions.

Adverb	Comparing Two	Comparing Three or More
gracefully		
soon		
quickly		
late		

Name: _____

60. Circle the adjective in parentheses that completes the sentence correctly.

1. The giraffe is the (taller / tallest) animal at the zoo.

2. On the (hotter / hottest) day in August, I went to the beach.

3. The pear is (juicier / juiciest) than the plum.

Prepositions

Name: _____

61. Underline the preposition in each sentence.

1. My friends and I went to the amusement park.

2. We rode on the roller coaster.

3. We rode a boat through the
   Tunnel of Terror.

Hint

A preposition shows the relationship of a noun or pronoun to another word in the sentence.

Prepositions

Name: _____

62. Write a preposition in the blank in each sentence.

1. On the Ferris wheel, we were high _____ the park.

2. My little brother sat _____ me on the roller coaster.

3. We had to pay admission _____ we went inside the park.

4. We climbed _____ a tram that took us to the parking lot.

Prepositions

Name: _____

63. Circle the prepositional phrases in the sentences below.

1. Friends threw beach balls across the pool.
2. The swimmers slid down the water chute.
3. The water splashed onto the swimmers.
4. Kids swam between the waterfalls.

Hint

A prepositional phrase starts with a preposition and ends with a noun or pronoun.

Prepositions

Name: _____

64. Complete each sentence with a prepositional phrase using a word from the box.

Prepositions
after
toward
above
with

1. We rode the Ferris wheel _____.

2. I ate an ice-cream cone _____.

3. At the end of the day, we headed _____.

Name: _____

65. Read the story below and fill in the blanks with prepositions.

Our family vacation was _____ July. We drove _____ the country from New York to California. Finally, we arrived _____ San Francisco. We rode the cable cars _____ the hills. We ate _____ a restaurant looking _____ the bay. The vacation was great!

Name: _____

66. Circle the conjunctions in the sentences below.

1. My favorite authors are J.K. Rowling and Jerry Spinelli.

2. I've read a lot of books, but I like their books best.

3. The last book I read was *Harry Potter and the Goblet of Fire*.

Hint

Conjunctions connect words or parts of sentences together.

Name: _____

67. Choose a conjunction from the box to connect the two short sentences. Then write the compound sentence.

Conjunctions

but
or
nor
and
so

1. I like to read mysteries. Lois Duncan is my favorite mystery author.

2. I like to read the books about Harry Potter. Some of them are too long.

3. I read sports books by Matt Christopher. I read a sports magazine.

Parts of Speech

Name: _____

68. Fill in each blank with a conjunction from the box.

Conjunctions

while
because
and
either/or
but
since

Tuck Everlasting is an outstanding book, _____ I think everyone should read it. One day, the main character named Winnie goes into a strange woods _____ she is running away from home. _____ she is in the woods, she meets a young man. He and his family kidnap her, _____ Winnie is not afraid of them. The Tuck family has not grown old ever _____ they drank from a magic spring. Winnie has to decide _____ to tell the Tucks' secret _____ to report them to the police. Read the book to find out what she decides!

Name: _____

69. Complete each compound sentence by adding a subject and predicate after the conjunction.

1. I won't start the fourth Harry Potter book until _____.
2. I read books by Lemony Snicket because _____.
3. I end up reading all night whenever _____.

Name: _____

70. Circle the six contractions in the story below.

We're having a bake sale in school tomorrow. It's to raise money for the local animal shelter. We'll have cookies, cupcakes, and brownies. So don't forget to stop by. You won't find better food anywhere. And you'll be glad you helped the animals, too.

Contractions

Name: _____

71. Write the two words that make up each contraction. Circle the letters that were dropped.

I'm _____ _____   he'd _____ _____   they're _____ _____

she's _____ _____   we've _____ _____   you'll _____ _____

Contractions

Name: _____

72. Fill in the blanks with contractions made from the words in parentheses.

(We are) _____ adopting a dog from the local animal shelter.

(She is) _____ part collie and part German shepherd. At the shelter,

(they will) _____ make sure our new dog is healthy and has her shots.

(I am) _____ in charge of walking her when we bring her home.

(That is) _____ my job as her new owner.

Contractions

Name: _____

73. Circle the six contractions in the story below.

Last night, the weatherman said we'd get lots of snow today. He's usually right, so I hoped for a snow day.

"There'll be no school tomorrow!" I yelled.

"You'd better wait and see," my mother warned.

This morning, there wasn't a bit of snow on the ground!

"That's unfair!" I said.

Parts of Speech

Name: _____

74. Fill in the missing words in the chart.

verb	+	not	=	contraction
are		not		
		not		shouldn't
has				
				won't

Name: _____

75. Write the two words that make up each contraction below. Then write if it is in the past, present, or future tense.

Contraction	they're	he'd	you're	I'll
Two Words				
Tense				

Name: _____

76. Write the two words that make up the contractions in each sentence.

1. There's always snow on the weekend when we don't have school!

2. There'll be a snow day if the roads are dangerous.

3. Who's the person with the authority to call off school?

Name: _____

77. Write a sentence using the contraction for each pair of words.

1. have not _____

2. you are _____

3. we have _____

4. she is _____

Name: _____

78. Underline the compound word in each sentence. Then write C for closed, O for open, or H for hyphenated.

_____ 1. We waded barefoot into the water.

_____ 2. The instructor made sure we had on life preservers.

_____ 3. There were twenty-one students in the class.

_____ 4. We got in the rowboats and picked up the oars.

Name: _____

79. Combine a word from the left column with a word from the right column to make five closed compound words.

1. flash	a. back
2. green	b. down
3. paper	c. mate
4. touch	d. light
5. class	e. house

Parts of Speech

Compound Words

Name: _____

80. Circle the open compounds in the sentences below.

1. My brother acts in the theater at the high school.

2. I went to the box office to buy tickets.

3. My brother got out of study hall to meet me.

Hint

Open compound words are written separately but have a shared meaning.

Compound Words

Name: _____

81. Add hyphens to the compound words in this story.

The evening was hot, so I was glad the theater was air conditioned. The play was a full length version of the book. My brother played a left handed pitcher on a baseball team. The narrator gave a play by play description of the games. Afterward, we went to a drive in restaurant to celebrate.

Review

Name: _____

82. Write a list of nouns, verbs, and adjectives. Start the next word with the last letter of the word before it.

Nouns	Verbs	Adjectives
dish	help	pretty

Name: _____

83. List five nouns that can be found at the beach.

_____ _____ _____ _____ _____

List five verbs that describe actions related to sports.

_____ _____ _____ _____ _____

List five plural pronouns.

_____ _____ _____ _____ _____

Name: _____

84. In the sentences below, identify the part of speech for each underlined word.

Parts of Speech
noun
verb
adjective

1. The neighbors got a <u>permit</u> for the block party. _____

2. My twin brothers are in <u>separate</u> classes. _____

3. I want to <u>house</u> my bicycle in the basement. _____

4. Our parents <u>permit</u> us to stay up late on Friday night. _____

5. I <u>separate</u> my notes for each subject. _____

Name: _____

85. Fill in a word in each blank. Then write its part of speech.

1. We rode on the _____ to the museum. _____

2. A guide _____ us about the dinosaurs. _____

3. The dinosaur bones were _____. _____

4. We were _____ interested in the exhibit. _____

Name: _____

86. Create original sentences by filling in the blanks with the correct part of speech.

1. _____ _____ _____ .
   Pronoun   verb   noun

2. _____ _____ _____ _____ _____ .
   Proper noun   verb   article   adjective   noun

3. _____ _____ _____ _____ _____ .
   Article   adjective   noun   verb   adverb

Name: _____

87. For each sentence below, write S if it is a statement, Q if it is a question, E if it is an exclamation, or C if it is a command.

_____ 1. What happened to the cookies I baked?

_____ 2. They were on the table a few minutes ago.

_____ 3. Did you eat them?

_____ 4. No, I did not!

Name: _____

88. Write the correct punctuation after each sentence.

1. Why are you late for school this morning

2. I was looking for my lost hamster

3. Are you telling the truth

4. I really am

5. Eek, here's my hamster

Types of Sentences

Name: _____

89. Answer each question with a statement or an exclamation.

1. Would you like to have a snake as a pet?

_____

2. What kind of animal do you think makes the best pet?

_____

3. Why should people adopt pets from an animal shelter?

_____

Types of Sentences

Name: _____

90. Rewrite each sentence below as a question.

1. Cats are harder to train than dogs.

_____

2. People have monkeys for pets in some countries.

_____

3. Dogs have to be walked twice a day.

_____

Subjects & Predicates

Name: _____

91. In each sentence, underline the simple subject—the noun or pronoun that tells who or what the sentence is about.

1. My family went to Yosemite National Park this summer.

2. We climbed a trail to the top of a waterfall.

3. At night, bears roamed around our tent.

4. I had the best vacation ever!

Name: _____

92. In each sentence, circle the simple predicate—the verb that tells what the subject does or is.

1. The rangers warn people about the bears.

2. The bears break into cars to get food.

3. Food attracts bears to a campsite.

4. Campers keep their food in sealed containers.

Name: _____

93. Draw a line to connect each subject with a matching predicate to make a complete sentence.

Subject	Predicate
1. Our school's field day	a. gets blue ribbons.
2. The three-legged race	b. is held in the spring.
3. The winning team	c. is run by two people together.

Name: _____

94. Complete each sentence by adding a subject or a predicate.

1. A softball team from each class _____.

2. _____ lasts for three innings.

3. The winner of each game _____.

Name: _____

95. Write a complete sentence using each phrase below.

1. my favorite sport

_____

2. the best snack in the world

_____

3. on a hot day

_____

Name: _____

96. Write S if the statement is a complete sentence or F if it's a sentence fragment.

_____ 1. The girls ran faster than the boys did this year.

_____ 2. The coach of our team.

_____ 3. Our teachers cheered for us in the race.

_____ 4. We won.

Name: _____

97. Rewrite the words below to unscramble the sentences. Add the correct punctuation.

1. won My last championship class year the

_____

2. fastest were We the and strongest the

_____

3. do think Who will this you year win

_____

Name: _____

98. Underline the subject and circle the verb in each sentence. Write A if the verb agrees with the subject. Write N if it does not agree.

_____ 1. Massachusetts are a state in New England.

_____ 2. The capital of Massachusetts is Boston.

_____ 3. The early settlers of Massachusetts was Puritans.

_____ 4. Boston has many historical sites.

Name: _____

99. Circle the correct verb form for each sentence.

1. People (love / loves) to go to Florida for vacation.

2. The South (has / have) warm weather in the winter.

3. Oranges and grapefruits (grow / grows) in Florida.

4. My family (go / goes) to Disney World every spring.

Name: _____

100. Fill in each blank with a verb that agrees with the subject of the sentence.

My family and I _____ big fans of Arizona. The desert there

_____ beautiful. Huge cactuses _____ to over 10

feet high. A road _____ through amazing rock formations.

We _____ lots of pictures.

Name: _____

101. Circle the correct verb form for each pronoun subject.

1. We (like / likes) to visit San Francisco.

2. It (seem / seems) like the most exciting city in the country.

3. We (stay / stays) with my aunt.

4. She (live / lives) on top of a hill near the cable cars.

Name: _____

102. Finish the sentences below, using a verb that agrees with the subject.

1. My part of the country _____ .

2. In the winter, we _____ .

3. In the summer, it _____ .

Name: _____

103. Circle the correct verb form for the sentences below.

1. The team (is / are) ready to play.

2. That flock of birds (flies / fly) over my house each afternoon.

3. Our class of seventh-graders (has / have) to clean the cafeteria.

Hint

Use a singular verb after a collective noun because the group usually acts as a single unit.

Name: _____

104. Write a verb for each sentence.

1. My brother and my sister _____ soccer.

2. Eric and Josh _____ in the school choir.

3. The cats and dogs _____ together in the park.

Hint

Use a plural verb with compound subjects joined by *and*.

Name: _____

105. Circle the correct verb form for each sentence.

1. The pitcher or the shortstop (is / are) the best player.

2. A zebra or a giraffe (has / have) the most interesting fur.

3. Jessie or Kye (run / runs) the fastest in the class.

Hint

Use a singular verb with compound subjects joined by *or*.

Name: _____

106. Some indefinite pronouns are singular, some are plural, some are both. Read the sentences and write C for correct and I for incorrect.

Singular	Plural	Plural or Singular
anything	both	all
everyone	few	any
each	several	most

_____ 1. A few of the books are too boring to read.

_____ 2. Everyone think the teacher is great.

_____ 3. Anything is better than nothing.

_____ 4. Several of my friends is going to the movies.

Name: _____

107. In the blank before each sentence, write an S if it is a simple sentence. Write a C if it is a compound sentence.

_____ 1. Volcanoes can erupt without warning, and they can cause great damage.

_____ 2. Mount Saint Helens in the state of Washington erupted in 1980.

_____ 3. Lava destroyed many trees, and volcanic ash filled the sky.

_____ 4. Scientists try to warn people about volcanic eruptions, but volcanoes still give us big surprises.

Name: _____

108. Underline the two subjects and circle the two predicates in the compound sentences below. Put a box around the joining word—*or, and,* or *but.*

1. Deer nibbled at the grass, and coyotes hunted for prey.

2. The sun was bright in the sky, but the wind was cold and brisk.

3. Visitors can climb on the trails, or they can take a guided bus tour.

Name: _____

109. Complete each compound sentence by adding another simple sentence after the joining word.

1. I liked sleeping in the tent, but _____.

2. My mother cooked eggs over the fire, and _____.

3. We could buy a T-shirt for a souvenir, or _____.

Name: _____

110. Circle the conjunction *and*, *or*, or *but*, and place a comma in front of it.

1. Many islands in the Pacific Ocean were formed by volcanoes and more are still being created.

2. The Hawaiian islands were formed by volcanoes and there are active volcanoes there today.

3. Visitors to the big island of Hawaii can see an active volcano but they have to be careful where they walk.

Name: _____

111. Combine the two simple sentences to make a compound sentence.

1. Hot lava can knock down trees. It can set buildings on fire.

_____

2. Magma is molten rock inside a volcano. It is called lava when it comes out.

_____

Name: _____

112. Put a check beside each sentence that is a complex sentence.

Hint
A complex sentence has an independent clause joined with a dependent clause.

_____ 1. After the volcano erupted, a blanket of ash covered the town.

_____ 2. Lava flowed down the mountain in a fiery river.

_____ 3. The people were trapped until a helicopter picked them up.

Name: _____

113. Rewrite this run-on sentence as a complex sentence.

We saw a volcano erupting we were flying across the Pacific Ocean.

_____

_____

Rewrite this run-on sentence as a compound sentence.

Scientists try to predict volcanic eruptions they
aren't always successful.

_____

_____

Rewrite this run-on sentence as two simple sentences.

Volcanoes in the ocean can cause tsunamis they are huge waves of water.

_____

_____

Name: _____

114. Follow the directions to build sentences from this sentence starter: Carlos ran.
Add an adverb.

_____

Add another subject.

_____

Add a prepositional phrase.

_____

Name: _____

115. Rewrite the words below to unscramble the sentences. Add the correct punctuation.

1. for Run life your

_____

2. you that Did see monster

_____

3. think imagination wild your I going is

_____

Name: _____

116. Rewrite the words below to unscramble the sentences. Add the capitalization and end punctuation.

1. on grandmother my farm lives a working

_____

2. harvests of vegetables plenty she fresh

_____

3. salad a it's she thing likes eat to good

_____

Name: _____

117. Complete the thoughts below to create complex sentences.

1. While we were at the monster movie, _____.

2. _____ until I heard the screams.

3. After the movie was over, _____.

Name: _____

118. Write a simple sentence about a movie you have seen.

_____

Write a compound sentence about two of your favorite TV shows.

_____

Write a complex sentence about a favorite book.

_____

Name: _____

119. Capitalize the first word in a sentence and the pronoun *I* in the story below.

    i like to play computer games with my friends. we spend four hours every Friday night playing our favorite games. my parents say i spend too much time staring at a computer screen. i think it's a great way to pass time, and my eye-hand coordination is excellent!

Name: _____

120. Reading from left to right, find the proper nouns below. Circle the letters that should be capitalized, then write them on the blanks to spell another proper noun.

minnesota	bicycle	isabel sinclair	sweden
grass	iowa	sam simpson	trumpet
illinois	democracy	paris	computer
ink	peter	train	india

____ ____ ____ ____ ____ ____ ____ ____ ____ ____ ____ ____

Name: _____

121. Fill in the capital letters to complete the chart.

Proper Noun	Proper Adjective
America	___ merican
Japan	___ apanese
Europe	___ uropean
New York	___ ew ___ orker

Hint

Proper adjectives that come from proper nouns should be capitalized.

Name: _____

122. Complete the sentences below, using correct capitalization.

1. My favorite holiday is in the month of _____.

2. My favorite day of the week is _____.

3. I like the weather best during the season of _____.

4. This year my birthday is on a _____ in the month of _____.

Hint

Capitalize the days of the week and the months, but not the names of the seasons.

Name: _____

123. Circle 10 letters that should be capitalized because they are in the names of places.

Dear Kamil,

   Today we drove from taos, new mexico, to flagstaff, arizona. We passed through the sierra madre mountains. Then we drove across the painted desert. The cactuses are incredible!

                    Wish you were here,

                    Deena

Name: _____

124. Circle 10 letters that should be capitalized because they are in the names of geographical locations or holidays.

Dear Jennifer,

I hope you can visit sometime between halloween and thanksgiving. Maybe you could even visit new york city during the thanksgiving day parade. We could watch as the floats go down broadway. Later, we could look at the christmas decorations.

Come soon,
Leah

Name: _____

125. Fill in the chart with the missing country or nationality. Use a capital letter to begin each word.

Country	Nationality
	French
Russia	
	Mexican
India	

Name: _____

126. Find the names of planets below. Circle each letter that should be capitalized.

What would a trip through the solar system be like? You might start on mercury and then fly to venus. Next stop would be earth and then mars. Going farther out into space, you would see jupiter and saturn. Finally, in the far distance you could spy neptune.

Mechanics

Name: _____

127. Fill in the first letter of each month's name. Capitalize the first letter.

___ anuary   ___ ebruary   ___ arch   ___ pril

___ ay   ___ une   ___ uly   ___ ugust

___ eptember   ___ ctober   ___ ovember   ___ ecember

Name: _____

128. Find the seven days of the week below. Circle the letter that should be capitalized.

On monday after school I go to soccer practice. When tuesday comes, I head off to my drums lesson. On wednesday I have to go to the orthodontist to have my braces checked. On thursday it's soccer practice again. Every friday my friends and I play a neighborhood softball game. On saturday morning I have a soccer game. But sunday is my day of rest.

Name: _____

129. Circle the words that should start with a capital letter below.

Hint
Capitalize the first letter in words that describe historical periods or historical events.

1. Americans won their independence in the revolutionary war.

2. Thomas Jefferson drafted the declaration of independence.

3. Ulysses S. Grant and Robert E. Lee were generals in the civil war.

Name: _____

130. Circle the three family-member names that should be capitalized because they're being directly spoken to or about.

"Where did you put my homework, mom?" I asked.

"I didn't touch it," she answered. "Ask your sister."

"Did you move my homework, sis?" I asked.

"Not me," my sister said. "I'll bet dad moved it."

Name: _____

131. Circle the words that should be capitalized.

monday	girl	river	world war I
star	april	friday	country
brother	october	civil war	year
the constitution	history	ship	grandpa jones

Name: _____

132. Write an S for every sentence that is a statement. Write a C if the sentence is a command. Put a period after each sentence.

_____ 1. Our class went on a camping trip to the woods

_____ 2. Pitch your tents around the campfire

_____ 3. Don't get too close to the flames

_____ 4. The fire kept us warm at night

Name: _____

133. Write a question for each answer below. Don't forget the question mark.

1. _____
   I heard something in the woods.

2. _____
   Maybe it is a bear.

3. _____
   No, I think you should go first.

Name: _____

134. Underline the sentence in each pair that is an exclamation. Then add the correct punctuation to each sentence.

1. Is that a bear   Look out, it's a bear

2. Run for your life   We got away quickly

3. That bear was huge   Bears are brown or black

Name: _____

135. Fill in each space with a period, a question mark, or an exclamation point.

"Are you ready for a hike__" our teacher asked.

"We're ready__" we all yelled.

We started out through the woods__

"Ouch__" I screamed.

"What's the matter__" our teacher asked.

I explained, "I think something bit my leg__"

Commas

Hint

Add commas to separate parts of addresses and places.

Name: _____

136. Add commas to the sentences below. The first is done for you.

1. Our school can be found at 35 North Pleasant Avenue, Ridgewood, Ohio.

2. My best friend lives at 88 Colonial Road Ottawa Ohio.

3. Go to 222 Demarest Avenue Hohokus Ohio for great ice cream.

Commas

Hint

Add a comma after the day of the week, the number of the day, and the year when the sentence continues.

Name: _____

137. Write two sentences about important dates in your life.

Our school held its graduation ceremony on Tuesday, June 10, 2003, in the auditorium.

1. _____

2. _____

Commas

Hint

Add commas to separate three or more items in a series. Include a comma before the word *and*.

Name: _____

138. Add eight commas to the story below.

I went to my favorite ice-cream parlor with my friends Lisa Keesha Luis and Jake. The flavors of the day were chocolate peach fudge and caramel. I ordered chocolate ice cream with sprinkles coconut and peanuts on top. It was great!

MechanicS

Name: _____

139. Read each phrase below. Add a comma if needed and put a C in the blank.

_____ 1. the shiny new bicycle

_____ 2. a chocolate ice cream

_____ 3. a cuddly little kitten

_____ 4. a talented graceful dancer

Hint

Add a comma between two adjectives when they describe the same noun. Do not add a comma if the second adjective and the noun go together.

Commas

Name: _____

140. Answer the questions with sentences using commas.

1. On what date were you born?

_____

2. In what city or town does your cousin live?

_____

3. What are the names of three of your classmates?

_____

Colons & Semicolons

Name: _____

141. Complete each sentence with a colon followed by a list of items.

1. I have to pack many things in my gym bag

_____ .

2. For dinner we had all my favorite foods

_____ .

3. These are the toppings I like on my pizza

_____ .

Hint

Use a colon to introduce a list after an independent clause.

Name: _____

142. Add colons to the schedule below.

Camp Crunch: Morning Schedule

Introduction to Getting in Shape	9 00 to 9 55
Stretching and Getting Ready	10 00 to 10 30
Jogging and Sprints	10 30 to 11 00
Using Muscle Machines	11 00 to 11 45

Hint Use a colon to separate the hour from the minutes when you write the time of day.

Name: _____

143. Add the missing colons below.

Dear Sirs:
Dear Senator Potter
To: Jason
From   Keesha
Date   May 12, 2003
Subject   6th-Grade Graduation

Hint Use a colon after the greeting in a business letter and after the headings in a memo.

Name: _____

144. Add a semicolon and comma in the sentences below. Use the first sentence as a model.

Antonio is a great basketball player; however, he can't play on the team because he works after school.

1. Our dog needs to be walked four times a day consequently my mother comes home for lunch to walk him.
2. I really want a new bicycle therefore I'm doing odd jobs to earn money.

Hint Use a semicolon before certain conjunctions that join independent clauses in a compound sentence. Put a comma after the conjunction.

Dialogue

Name: _____

145. Read the dialogue below. Draw a line under the words that are spoken. Circle the person who is speaking.

"Did you see the new movie *Alien Attack*?" asked Tonya.

"I saw it last night," Roberto said. "It was great!"

"You call that a great movie?" Tonya exclaimed. "I thought the aliens looked like people in bad Halloween masks!"

Roberto answered, "Maybe that's what aliens look like!"

Dialogue

Name: _____

146. Read each piece of dialogue below. Add the missing quotation marks around the words that are spoken.

Tonya said, Those aliens had faces that looked like rubber masks!

But their costumes were great, Roberto said. I liked the uniforms the alien soldiers wore.

You're right about that, Tonya agreed. The battle scene was really scary.

Dialogue

Name: _____

147. Read each piece of dialogue. Then write a dialogue response on the line below.

"What is your favorite science-fiction movie?" Tonya asked.

_____

"Which *Star Wars* movie did you like best?" Roberto asked.

_____

Name: _____

148. Add the missing quotation marks, commas, periods, question marks, and exclamation points to the dialogue below.

Halt the guard said Who are you and where are you going

Take me to your leader the strange creature said

Only aliens say that the guard responded nervously

Name: _____

149. Underline the six book titles in the paragraph below.

    If you want to read a great book about horses, try Black Beauty. Or if you like to read books about dogs, try either Sounder or Shiloh. Stuart Little is about a mouse and Charlotte's Web is about a spider and a pig. Another great book about a pig is Babe.

Hint

Underline the titles of books when writing. (Use italics on a computer.)

Name: _____

150. Underline the titles of the newspapers and magazines in the sentences below.

1. My sister's favorite magazine is Sports Illustrated for Kids.

2. My brother likes to read SuperScience.

3. I like to read the comics in the Daily News.

Name: _____

151. Underline the titles of the movies and television shows in the dialogue below.

"Did you watch Survivor last night on television?"

"No, I was watching Star Wars on our DVR."

"Did you like it as much as Lord of the Rings?"

"Yes, and then I watched Star Trek on television."

Name: _____

152. Add quotation marks to the titles below. Then add examples of your own.

Song	Yellow Submarine	_____
Book Chapter	Help Is on the Way	_____
Article	How to Skateboard	_____
Poem	The Raven	_____

Hint

Use quotation marks around the titles of songs, chapters in a book, magazine articles, and poems.

Name: _____

153. Write an abbreviation from the box in each blank. Don't forget the period at the end of each abbreviation.

Abbreviations

Dr.
Capt.
Ms.

1. When I broke my finger playing softball, my coach, _____ Ross, called 911 on her cell phone.

2. The police rushed to the field, and _____ Russell took me to the hospital.

3. At the hospital, _____ Bauer set my finger in a cast.

Name: _____

154. Write the abbreviation for each word on the left. Then write the name of a specific place using the abbreviation. An example is done for you.

Word	Abbreviation	Example
Road	Rd.	Cedar Rd.
Street		
Avenue		
Drive		

Abbreviations

Name: _____

155. Write the abbreviations for the following days of the week and months of the year.

Monday	_____	January	_____
Tuesday	_____	February	_____
Wednesday	_____	August	_____
Thursday	_____	September	_____
Friday	_____	October	_____
Saturday	_____	November	_____
Sunday	_____	December	_____

Abbreviations

Name: _____

156. Write the word that each of the following abbreviations stands for.

Co.	_____	ft.	_____
in.	_____	Jr.	_____
km.	_____	oz.	_____
Pres.	_____	qt.	_____
Sen.	_____	yd.	_____

Review

Name: _____

157. Add correct capitalization and punctuation to the sentences below.

1. where are you going on vacation this summer

2. i have a job working at sunnyside country club

3. we ll have to carpool together from ridgewood to our jobs

Mechanics

Review

Name: _____

158. Add quotation marks and correct punctuation to the dialogue below.

How long have you been swimming the coach asked

I started to swim when I was 6 Merri answered

Do you think you can work with young children the coach asked

I would love to teach them to swim Merri said

Review

Name: _____

159. Circle the first letter of each word in the list that should be capitalized.

summer	american	january	bicycle
monday	italian	soccer	sister
civil war	comma	friday	halloween
computer	saturn	ohio	dr. russell

Review

Name: _____

160. Check each sentence that has correct capitalization and punctuation.

_____ 1. "Mom, where are my new jeans?" Dana asked.

_____ 2. These are my party guests; Luis, Marisol, Jenny and Mike.

_____ 3. Meet me at Mario's Pizza at 6:15 on Monday.

Review

Name: _____

161. Add the correct capitalization and punctuation to the paragraph below.

My friends and I met at mario's pizza last monday after soccer practice. The Restaurant is on central avenue near main street in dayton We asked for pizza with the works; cheese, mushrooms, pepperoni and sausage? The smell was outstanding and the taste was even better. it was one great pizza?

Name: _____

162. Check each sentence that contains a double negative.

_____ 1. My family doesn't believe in polluting the environment.

_____ 2. We don't never throw away glass bottles.

_____ 3. The environment will never get better without recycling!

Name: _____

163. Circle the correct word to complete each sentence.

1. Pollution shouldn't (never / ever) be allowed.

2. Many fish (can / can't) hardly survive in polluted rivers.

3. Pesticides shouldn't be used (anywhere / nowhere) around endangered wildlife.

Name: _____

164. Match each negative word in the left column with its positive opposite.

Negative Word	Positive Opposite
1. nobody	a. either
2. neither	b. something
3. none	c. anybody
4. nothing	d. some

Name: _____

165. Rewrite each sentence to correct the double negative.

1. We don't never waste paper in our classroom.

2. We don't throw away aluminum cans neither.

3. Nobody in the class hardly never uses Styrofoam cups.

USage

Name: _____

166. Cross out some words in the story to correct the double negatives.

Our class volunteered at the recycling center last Saturday. We didn't hardly know how much work it would be! A lot of kids had not never been there before. We helped people carry their newspapers, bottles, and cans to the recycling bins. Recycling isn't no easy work, but it is worth it!

Homophones

Name: _____

167. Put a check after each pair of words that are homophones.

so / sew _____   daze / days _____

accept / except _____   sum / some _____

which / witch _____   then / than _____

though / through _____   bear / bare _____

Hint

Homophones are words that sound alike but have different meanings.

Homophones

Name: _____

168. Circle the correct homophone to complete each sentence.

1. My new bicycle has (eight / ate) speeds.

2. It is (blew / blue) with red trim.

3. I can't (weight / wait) to ride my bike to school.

Homophones

Name: _____

169. Circle six incorrect homophones below and replace them with the correct words.

"I asked for a pear of in-line skates for my birthday. At first, my parents said, "Know weigh!" But I one them over when I promised to where a helmet and knee guards. Now I can do sum awesome tricks on my skates.

Homophones

Name: _____

170. Complete each sentence by filling in a homophone of the underlined word.

1. My <u>two</u> friends and I went _____ a skateboard store.

2. We saw <u>some</u> skateboards that cost a huge _____ of money.

3. We knew it was too big of a <u>feat</u> to get our _____ on those boards.

Easily Confused Words

Name: _____

171. Circle the correct word in each sentence.

1. Did (you're / your) mom sign the permission slip?

2. (You're / Your) a talented and dedicated athlete.

3. I smile when (you're / your) dog wags its tail.

Hint
The word *you're* is a contraction for "you are." The word *your* is a possessive pronoun.

Easily Confused Words

Name: _____

172. Write C for correct or I for incorrect for each sentence.

_____ 1. There were bad feelings between my sister and me.

_____ 2. We divided the candy between the five children.

_____ 3. We divided the cost of the gift among Sandy, Liz, and me.

Hint
The word *between* is a preposition used when there are two people or things. *Among* is used when there are more than two of something.

Name: _____

173. Circle the correct word in each sentence.

1. My dog lost (it's / its) bone.
2. I think (it's / its) a funny movie.
3. When the bell rings, (it's / its) time to go home.
4. Our class had (it's / its) first field trip yesterday.

Hint
The word *it's* is a contraction for "it is." The word *its* is a possessive pronoun.

Name: _____

174. Write either *good* or *well* in each blank.

1. He performed _____ in the class play.

2. The dinner after the play was very _____.

3. The school newspaper wrote that it was a _____ production.

Hint
The word *good* describes a noun or pronoun. The word *well* describes a verb.

Name: _____

175. Circle the correct words in each sentence.

1. (You're / Your) study habits helped you do (good / well) on the test.

2. (It's / Its) not easy to choose (among / between) vanilla and chocolate ice cream.

Name: _____

176. Match the easily confused word pairs with their definitions.

1. accept   a. to take what is offered
2. except   b. leaving out
3. affect   c. a result or consequence
4. effect   d. to influence or change

Name: _____

177. Circle the correct word to complete each sentence.

1. My mother made me do a (thorough / through) cleaning of my room.

2. I even had to throw away some (personnel / personal) letters I had received.

3. Over the years, I've had to (adapt / adopt) to my mother's neatness.

Name: _____

178. Circle the word at right that fits with each phrase.

1. a baseball game   empire   umpire

2. no noise   quiet   quite

3. a taste like sugar   suite   sweet

4. misplace   loose   lose

Name: _____

179. Read each sentence and think about the meaning of the underlined word. Then write T for true or F for false.

_____ 1. A <u>dessert</u> is a hot, dry, sandy region.

_____ 2. An <u>alley</u> is a narrow street or passageway.

_____ 3. A <u>magnate</u> is a piece of metal that attracts iron.

Name: _____

180. Circle the correct word to complete each sentence.

1. Henry poured orange juice from the (pitcher / picture).

2. Our (principal / principle) greeted students at the school's main entrance.

3. On vacation, we visited a historic (cite / site).

Answers

1. Person: fans, girl, coach, runner, Venus Williams; Place: city, outfield, Chicago, Europe; Thing: baseball, net, medal, hurdle

2. 1. brother, soccer, tennis 2. batter, ball, park 3. team, court, fans

3. 1. Michael Jordan, basketball player 2. runner, Kenya 3. Mia Hamm, athletes

4. Heroes, Odds, crowd, Kyle Ellis, youngster, team, Eagles, nationals, Newport, invitation, soccer, team, record, athletes, championship, Kyle; hockey, tennis, track

5. 1. P 2. S 3. P 4. S 5. S 6. S 7. P 8. S 9. S or P 10. S

6. 1. zoo, S 2. People, P 3. elephant, S

7. 1. brothers 2. foxes 3. bushes 4. gorillas

8. 1. keys 2. leaves 3. knives 4. monkeys

9. 1. d 2. e 3. b 4. a 5. c

10. 1. The lions walked back and forth in the cages. 2. The foxes ran past the trees and into the bushes. 3. The children tossed balls into the hoops.

11. 1. He 2. It 3. They

12. 1. her, singer 2. their, members 3. our, We 4. your, You

13. 1. c 2. e 3. f 4. a 5. b 6. d

14. 1. us 2. he 3. I 4. she

15. she, S; they, P; his, S; we, P Sentences will vary.

16. She, their, her, It

17. 1. I; We like the comics section of the newspaper best. 2. her; Teresa asked them to cover the soccer game. 3. He; They write the humor column for the newspaper.

18. 1. his 2. our 3. her 4. its

19. 1. airplane 2. Wilbur and Orville Wright 3. jets

20. Answers will vary.

21. me; you; he; her; it; we; them

22. 1, We, S 2. her, O 3. She, S

23. 1. They were aviation pioneers. 2. She was the first American woman in space. 3. He walked on the moon.

24. 1. audience, band 2. choir 3. class

25. 1. c 2. d 3. a 4. e 5. b

26. hamster's; quarterback's; bike's; girl's; dogs'; runners'; motorcycles'; boys'

27. 1. mice's 2. geese's 3. children's

28. 1. coaches', P 2. boys', P 3. women's, P 4. referee's, S

29. 1. ripped 2. pounded 3. rumbled

30. Answers will vary.

31. 1. is moving 2. are bending 3. can hear

32. 1. are, main 2. am, helping 3. are, main

33. tore, wrecked, interrupted, streamed, trembled, emerged, ran; twister

34. 1. present 2. past 3. future

35. 1. ride 2. perform 3. takes

36. 1. The boy fell off his skateboard. 2. Luckily, he was wearing safety equipment. 3. He got back up and skated on down the street.

37. All answers: will

38. sat; found; told. Sentences will vary.

39. 1. went 2. sang 3. stole

40. 1. saw 2. spoke 3. flew 4. kept

41. spoke; ring, rung; did, done

42. Sentences will vary.

43. huge, what kind; that, which one; four, how many; green, what kind

44. Answers will vary.

45. 1. three 2. most 3. two 4. several

46. 1. this, that 2. these 3. those

47. quickly, impatiently, great, high, never

48. Answers will vary.

49. 1. yesterday, when 2. everywhere, where 3. downstairs, where 4. always, when

50. How: gently, fast, slowly, easily; Where: near, here, inside, up; When: never, often, tomorrow, finally

51. extremely, really, very, too

52. 1. very 2. extremely 3. too 4. quite

53. softly, loudly, awkwardly, foolishly, beautifully, happily

54. 1. greedily, verb 2. extremely, adjective 3. very, adverb

55. 1. c 2. d 3. a 4. e 5. b

56. 1. more 2. more 3. most

57. faster, fastest; more athletic, most athletic; more expensive, most expensive; newer, newest

58. 1. hardest 2. higher 3. fastest 4. louder

59. more gracefully, most gracefully; sooner, soonest; more quickly, most quickly; later, latest

60. 1. tallest 2. hottest 3. juicier

61. 1. to 2. on 3. through

62. Answers will vary.

63. 1. across the pool 2. down the water chute 3. onto the swimmers 4. between the waterfalls

64. Answers will vary.

65. Answers will vary.

66. 1. and 2. but 3. and

67. 1. I like to read mysteries, and Lois Duncan is my favorite mystery author. 2. I like to read books about Harry Potter, but some of them are too long. 3. I read sports books by Matt Christopher, or I read a sports magazine.

68. and; because; While; but; since; either; or

69. Answers will vary.

70. We're; It's; We'll; don't; won't; you'll

71. I am; he had; they are; she is; we have; you will

72. We're; She's; they'll; I'm; That's

73. we'd; He's; There'll; You'd; wasn't; That's

74. aren't; should; not, hasn't; will, not

75. they are, present; he had, past; you are, present; I will, future

76. 1. There is, do not 2. There will 3. Who is

77. 1. haven't 2. you're 3. we've 4. she's Sentences will vary.

78. 1. barefoot, C 2. life preservers, O 3. twenty-one, H 4. rowboats, C

79. 1. d 2. e 3. a 4. b 5. c

80. 1. high school 2. box office 3. study hall

81. air-conditioned; full-length; left-handed; play-by-play; drive-in

82. Answers will vary.

83. Answers will vary.

84. 1. noun 2. adjective 3. verb 4. verb 5. verb

85. Answers will vary.

86. Sentences will vary.

87. 1. Q 2. S 3. Q 4. E

88. 1. ? 2. . 3. ? 4. . or ! 5. !

89. Sentences will vary.

90. 1. Are cats harder to train than dogs? 2. Do people have monkeys for pets in some countries? 3. Do dogs have to be walked twice a day?

91. 1. family 2. We 3. bears 4. I

92. 1. warn 2. break 3. attracts 4. keep

93. 1. b 2. c 3. a

94. Answers will vary.

95. Sentences will vary.

96. 1. S 2. F 3. S 4. S

97. 1. My class won the championship last year. 2. We were the fastest and the strongest. 3. Who do you think will win this year?

98. 1. Massachusetts, are, N 2. capital, is, A 3. settlers, was, N 4. Boston, has, A

99. 1. love 2. has 3. grow 4. goes

100. Answers will vary.

101. 1. like 2. seems 3. stay 4. lives

102. Answers will vary.

103. 1. is 2. flies 3. has

104. Answers will vary.

105. 1. is 2. has 3. runs

106. 1. C 2. I 3. C 4. I

107. C, S, C, C

108. 1. Deer nibbled . . . and coyotes hunted 2. sun was . . . but wind was 3. Visitors can climb . . . or they can take

109. Answers will vary.

110. 1. and 2. and 3. but

111. 1. Hot lava can knock down trees, and it can set buildings on fire. 2. Magma is molten rock inside a volcano, but it is called lava when it comes out.

112. Check 1 and 3.

113. 1. As we were flying across the Pacific Ocean, we saw a volcano erupting. 2. Scientists try to predict volcanic eruptions, but they aren't always successful. 3. Volcanoes in the ocean can cause tsunamis. Tsunamis are huge waves of water.

114. Sentences will vary.

115. 1. Run for your life! 2. Did you see that monster? 3. I think your imagination is going wild.

116. 1. My grandmother lives on a working farm. 2. She harvests plenty of fresh vegetables. 3. It's a good thing she likes to eat salad.

117. Answers will vary.

118. Sentences will vary.

119. I, We, My, I, I

120. Minnesota, Isabel Sinclair, Sweden, Iowa, Sam Simpson, Illinois, Paris, Peter, India; Mississippi

121. American; Japanese; European; New Yorker

122. Answers will vary.

123. Taos, New Mexico, Flagstaff, Arizona, Sierra Madre Mountains, Painted Desert

124. Halloween, Thanksgiving, New York City, Thanksgiving Day Parade, Broadway, Christmas

125. France; Russian; Mexico; Indian

126. Mercury, Venus, Earth, Mars, Jupiter, Saturn, Neptune

127. January, February, March, April, May, June, July, August, September, October, November, December

128. Monday, Tuesday, Wednesday, Thursday, Friday, Saturday, Sunday

129. 1. Revolutionary War 2. Declaration of Independence 3. Civil War

130. Mom, Sis, Dad

131. Monday, World War I, April, October, Civil War, the Constitution, Grandpa Jones

132. 1. S 2. C 3. C 4. S

133. Questions will vary.

134. 1. Look out, it's a bear! 2. Run for your life! 3. That bear was huge!

135. ? ! . ! ? .

136. 2. My best friend lives at 88 Colonial Road, Ottawa, Ohio. 3. Go to 222 Demarest Avenue, Hohokus, Ohio, for great ice cream.

137. Sentences will vary.

138. I went to my favorite ice-cream parlor with my friends Lisa, Keesha, Luis, and Jake. The flavors of the day were chocolate, peach, fudge, and caramel. I ordered chocolate ice cream with sprinkles, coconut, and peanuts on top. It was great!

139. 1. C, the shiny, new bicycle 2. a chocolate ice cream 3. C, a cuddly, little kitten 4. C, a talented, graceful dancer

140. Answers will vary.

141. Answers will vary.

142. 9:00 to 9:55; 10:00 to 10:30; 10:30 to 11:00; 11:00 to 11:45

143. Potter:; From:; Date:; Subject:

144. 1. Our dog needs to be walked four times a day; consequently, my mother comes home for lunch to walk him. 2. I really want a new bicycle; therefore, I'm doing odd jobs to earn money.

145. "Did you see the new movie Alien Attack?" Tonya; "I saw it last night." Roberto "It was great!"; "You call that a great movie?" Tonya "I thought the aliens looked like people in bad Halloween masks!" Roberto "Maybe that's what aliens look like!"

146. 1. "Those aliens had faces that looked like rubber masks!" "But their costumes were great," "I liked the uniforms the alien soldiers wore." "You're right about that," "The battle scene was really scary."

147. Answers will vary.

148. "Halt!" the guard said. "Who are you and where are you going?" "Take me to your leader," the strange creature said. "Only aliens say that," the guard responded nervously.

149. Black Beauty, Sounder, Shiloh, Stuart Little, Charlotte's Web, Babe

150. Sports Illustrated for Kids, SuperScience, Daily News

151. Survivor, Star Wars, Lord of the Rings, Star Trek

152. "Yellow Submarine," "Help Is on the Way," "How to Skateboard," "The Raven." Examples will vary.

153. 1. Ms. 2. Capt. 3. Dr.

154. St.; Ave.; Dr. Examples will vary.

155. Mon., Tues., Wed., Thurs., Fri., Sat., Sun., Jan., Feb., Aug., Sept., Oct., Nov., Dec.

156. Company, inch, kilometer, President, Senator, foot, Junior, ounce, quart, yard

157. 1. Where are you going on vacation this summer? 2. I have a job working at Sunnyside Country Club. 3. We'll have to carpool together from Ridgewood to our jobs.

158. "How long have you been swimming?" the coach asked. "I started to swim when I was 6," Merri answered. "Do you think you can work with young children?" the coach asked. "I would love to teach them to swim!" Merri said.

159. American, January, Monday, Italian, Civil War, Friday, Halloween, Saturn, Ohio, Dr. Russell

160. Check 1 and 3.

161. My friends and I met at Mario's Pizza last Monday after soccer practice. The restaurant is on Central Avenue near Main Street in Dayton. We asked for pizza with the works: cheese, mushrooms, pepperoni, and sausage. The smell was outstanding, and the taste was even better. It was one great pizza!

162. Check 2.

163. 1. ever 2. can 3. anywhere

164. 1. c 2. a 3. d 4. b

165. 1. We never waste paper in our classroom. 2. We don't throw away aluminum cans either. 3. Nobody in the class ever uses Styrofoam cups.

166. hardly, not, no

167. so / sew, which / witch, daze / days, sum / some, bear / bare

168. 1. eight 2. blue 3. wait

169. pear / pair; Know / No; weigh / way; one / won; where / wear; sum /some

170. 1. to 2. sum 3. feet

171. 1. your 2. You're 3. your

172. 1. C 2. I 3. C

173. 1. its 2. it's 3. it's 4. its

174. 1. well 2. good 3. good

175. 1. Your, well 2. It's, between

176. 1. a 2. b 3. d 4. c

177. 1. thorough 2. personal 3. adapt

178. 1. umpire 2. quiet 3. sweet 4. lose

179. 1. F 2. T 3. F

180. 1. pitcher 2. principal 3. site